AMISH
WIT &
WISDOM

✳✳✳

Publications International, Ltd.

Friendship, Laughter, and Wisdom

✳✳✳

*"A merry heart doeth good like a medicine:
but a broken spirit drieth the bones."*

—**Proverbs 17:22**

O nce a month, extended Amish families gather. Every-one, happy to see each other, talks of their daily doings, their struggles, their triumphs, and lots of good-natured ribbing and laughter is heard throughout the evening.

After church service on Sunday, people stay for a fellowship meal. Many serious conversations are held, but again there is lots of laughter. In cozy Amish homes, most of the wit and wisdom is shared around the table during meals.

And don't be surprised to hear that the Amish have their share of practical jokers, too. Blessed are the jokers who can make people laugh in a good way—without hurting anyone's feelings.

Humor is often the way the Amish deliver their wisdom. Their wit is showcased in pithy sayings such as these:

✳ A smile is a curve that can straighten out a lot of things.

✳ The person who thinks too little usually talks too much.

Humor is an important part of every culture, and the Amish have certainly incorporated wisdom into theirs. Take their wit to heart, and add laughs and common sense to your life.

❋❋❋

He who has no money is poor; he who has nothing but money is even poorer.

❋❋❋

If you think you're too small to make a difference, you haven't been in bed with a mosquito.

❋❋❋

It is better to have a wife on your team than on your back.

❋❋❋

The reason some people get lost in thought is because it is unfamiliar territory.

✳✳✳

An industrious wife is the best savings account.

✳✳✳

Good deeds have echoes.

✳✳✳

A task takes as long as it takes.

✳✳✳

Blessed are they who have nothing to say and who cannot be persuaded to say it.

✳✳✳

You may as well borrow a person's money as his time.

✳✳✳

It is better to give others a piece of your heart than a piece of your mind.

✳✳✳

Fortune knocks once, but misfortune has more patience.

✳✳✳

There are no degrees of honesty.

✳✳✳

Swallowing words before you say them is so much better than having to eat them afterward.

✳✳✳

Summer is the season when children slam the doors they left open all winter.

✳✳✳

A sweater is a garment worn by a child when his mother feels chilly.

※※※

Medicine and advice are two things more pleasant to give than to receive.

※※※

Jumping for joy is good exercise.

※※※

Use it up, wear it out,
make it do, or do without.

※※※

One thing you can learn by watching the clock is that it passes time by keeping its hands busy.

※※※

Money talks, but it doesn't say when it will be back.

※※※

A man is rich in proportion to the things he can afford to leave alone.

✳✳✳

Beware of the man who knows the answer before he understands the question.

✳✳✳

Children are the living messages we send to a time we will not see.

✳✳✳

Community is like an old coat—you aren't aware of it until it is taken away.

✳✳✳

The light that shines farthest, shines brightest at home.

✳✳✳

In autumn sunshine, prepare for winter's cold.

✳✳✳

If you can't see the bright side, polish the dull.

✳✳✳

The secret to getting ahead is getting started.

✳✳✳

Anger makes your mouth work faster than
your mind.

✳✳✳

A full purse never lacks friends.

✳✳✳

Parents who are afraid to put their foot down
usually have children who step on their toes.

✳✳✳

A dollar saved is a dollar earned, but seldom
vice versa.

✳✳✳

Swallowing pride rarely gives you indigestion.

✳✳✳

Why is is so hard to say, "I broke it" and so easy to say, "it broke"?

✳✳✳

You are only poor when you want more than you have.

✳✳✳

Regrets over yesterday and the fear of tomorrow are twin thieves that rob us of the moment.

✳✳✳

The trouble with doing nothing is that it's too hard to tell when you're finished.

✳✳✳

The only time to look down on your neighbor is when you're bending over to help.

***

It isn't the mountains ahead that wear you out, it's the grain of sand in your shoe.

***

If you're careful with your pennies, the dollars will take care of themselves.

***

Learn from your failures, or you will fail to learn.

***

A house is made of walls and beams;
a home is made of love and dreams.

***

Laziness travels so slowly that poverty soon overtakes it.

***

He talked much but said little.

✳✳✳

The years can fly past like a flock of birds.

✳✳✳

If parents don't train their children, the children will train their parents.

✳✳✳

It is the set of the sails, and not the gales, that determines the path you go.

✳✳✳

There is no limit to what a man can do if he doesn't care who gets the credit.

✳✳✳

An unkind remark is like a killing frost—no matter how much it warms up, the damage is already done.

✳✳✳

People who reject law and order change their minds when they can lay down the laws and give the orders.

✳✳✳

A friend is like a rainbow, always here for you after a storm.

✳✳✳

Don't hurry, don't worry:
Do your best and leave the rest.

✳✳✳

The best vitamin for making friends is to B1.

✳✳✳

Advice when most needed is least heeded.

✳✳✳

Be contented, and do not try to catch up with the world's uneasiness and speed.

✳✳✳

There's only one way to fail, and that's to quit.

✳✳✳

Many times we are climbing mountains when we ought to be quietly resting.

✳✳✳

Start each day with a fresh beginning as if this whole world was made anew.

✳✳✳

Instead of complaining that the rosebush is full of thorns, be glad that the thornbush has roses.

✳✳✳

The most important things in your home are people.

✳✳✳

All that you do, do with all your might.
Things done by halves are never done right.

✳✳✳

The person who gets all wrapped up in himself
makes a mighty small package.

✳✳✳

There are lots of ways to cut a cake.

✳✳✳

I am only one, but I'm still someone.

✳✳✳

If you let your children have their own way, you
must not complain if they give you trouble.

✳✳✳

I cannot do everything, but I can still do something.

✳✳✳

Someday the scales of justice will be perfectly balanced.

✳✳✳

Keep your feet under your own table.

✳✳✳

Two cannot quarrel when one will not.

✳✳✳

Remember, when you talk you only repeat what you already know, but if you listen you may learn something.

✳✳✳

If the grass looks greener on the other side, fertilize.

✳✳✳

Teaching children to count is fine, but teaching them *what* counts is better.

✳✳✳

Do more of less.

✳✳✳

The soundness of your ideas is more important than the sound of your words.

✳✳✳

A truly happy person is one who can enjoy the scenery of a detour.

✳✳✳

Learning is far more valuable than education.

✳✳✳

A fault mender is better than a fault finder.

***

If we don't stand for something, we will fall for anything.

***

A thing long expected takes the form of the unexpected when it finally comes.

***

Raising boys is as easy as digesting iron.

***

If you put your finger to the fire, it will get burned.

***

We need old friends to help us grow old and new friends to help us stay young.

***

You can tell how big a person is by what it takes to discourage him.

✳✳✳

Opportunity may knock once, but temptation bangs on your front door forever.

✳✳✳

Those who have no children know best how to raise them.

✳✳✳

One can learn something new every day.

✳✳✳

Be kind to unkind people. They probably need kindness the most.

✳✳✳

We live simply so others may simply live.

✳✳✳

Trickles tend to become streams, and streams become torrents.

✳✳✳

Be like the teakettle. When it's up to its neck in hot water, it sings!

✳✳✳

Those who fear the future are likely to fumble the past.

✳✳✳

Too many people limit their exercise to jumping to conclusions, running up bills, stretching the truth, bending over backwards, lying down on the job, sidestepping responsibility, and pushing their luck.

✳✳✳

Tackle the problem, not the person.

✳✳✳

Kissing wears out, cooking don't.

***

We always admire the other fellow more after we
have tried to do his job.

***

The most beautiful attire is a smile.

***

If you are too big to do little things, you are probably
too little to be trusted with big things.

***

If you want life's best, see to it that life gets your best.

***

The person who thinks too little usually talks
too much.

***

Don't believe everything you think.

✳✳✳

Many things have been opened by mistake, but none so frequently as the mouth.

✳✳✳

A smile is a curve that can straighten out a lot of things.

✳✳✳

If you find a pathway with no obstacles, it probably doesn't lead anywhere.

✳✳✳

Mentioning the faults of others does not rid us of our own.

✳✳✳

Three are too many to keep a secret.

✳✳✳

Borrowing causes sorrowing.

✳✳✳

There is one thing more exasperating than a wife who can cook and won't, and that's a wife who can't cook and will.

✳✳✳

Your actions speak so loudly I can't hear a word you say.

✳✳✳

Those who can't forget are worse than those who can't remember.

✳✳✳

Encouragement is oxygen to the soul.

✳✳✳

Young folks should use their ears and not their mouths.

Our duty is not to see through one another, but to see one another through.

❋❋❋

He who talks to you about others will talk to others about you.

❋❋❋

Good character, like good soup, is usually homemade.

❋❋❋

Children are the poor man's wealth.

❋❋❋

He who has never done anything wrong has never done anything right.

❋❋❋

Every family tree has a little sap.

✳✳✳

Nothing is quite so annoying as having someone go right on talking when you are interrupting.

✳✳✳

You don't need to get sick to get better.

✳✳✳

Some people never learn anything because they understand everything too soon.

✳✳✳

Do you know what happens when you give a procrastinator a good idea? Nothing!

✳✳✳

The best way to escape from a problem is to solve it.

✳✳✳

Well begun is half done.

✳✳✳

If you listen through the wall, you'll hear others reciting your faults.

✳✳✳

Enthusiasm is contagious and so is the lack of it.

✳✳✳

Cheerfulness greases the axles of the world.

✳✳✳

It's what you learn after you know it all that counts.

✳✳✳

Before you flare up at anyone's faults, take time to count to ten—ten of your own.

✳✳✳

If you have done all you can, you've done enough.

※※※

An empty barrel makes the most noise.

※※※

A friend is never known till a man has need.

※※※

Those who have money are troubled about it,
those who have none are troubled without it.

※※※

The farther you go, the longer it takes to get back.

※※※

Enough is enough—more is too much.

❂❂❂

Health is the greatest wealth.

❂❂❂

When children are little, you have them on your lap;
when grown up, on your heart.

❂❂❂

If it costs nothing, it is not worth much.

❂❂❂

Let others praise you.

❂❂❂

Take all things as they come, and be content.

❂❂❂

Tell me who your friends are, and I will tell you who
you are.

✳✳✳

Too sharp is as bad as too dull.

✳✳✳

Be saving but not stingy, be liberal but not wasteful.

✳✳✳

Don't close your eyes if you want to see.

✳✳✳

There is sunshine also behind the clouds.

✳✳✳

Where ignorance is bliss it is folly to be wise.

✳✳✳

He knows much who knows that he knows nothing.

✳✳✳

What is not worth asking for is not worth having.